TREASURE!

Diana Bentley
and Sylvia Karavis

Story illustrated by
Tom Percival

Heinemann

Before Reading

Find out about

- How two men found the tomb of Tutankhamen

Tricky words

- Egypt
- treasure
- tomb
- mask
- found
- throne
- believe

Introduce these tricky words and help the reader when they come across them later!

Text starter

Tutankhamen was an Egyptian king who lived 3000 years ago. He died when he was only nineteen and all his treasure was buried with him. In 1916 two men, Lord Carnarvon and Howard Carter, went to Egypt to find the treasure.

The Search for the Treasure of Tutankhamen

Two men went to Egypt to find the treasure.
But first they had to find the tomb.
The tomb was under the sand.

Howard Carter

Lord Carnarvon

The men dug in the sand.
They dug and dug.
But they could not find
the tomb.

They dug in the sand for *six years!*
Then they found a door under the sand.
It was the door to the tomb.

How do you think the men felt when they found the door to the tomb?

They opened the door to
the tomb.
Then they went inside.
It was very dark.

Inside the tomb they found
a room.
They went inside the room
and found it was full of gold.

There was a gold bed, a gold mask and a gold throne.
The two men could not believe their eyes!

All the rooms in the tomb
were full of treasure.
The two men could not believe
how much gold there was
in the tomb.

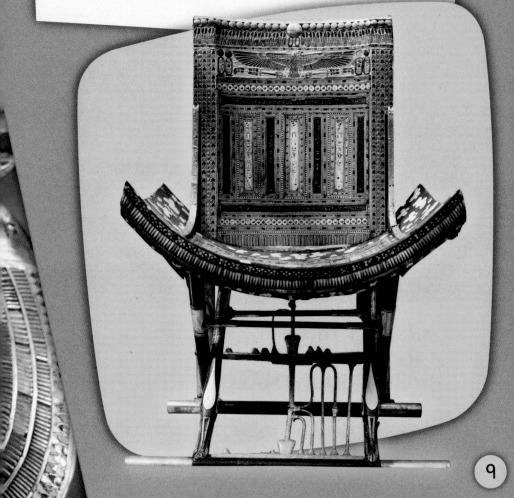

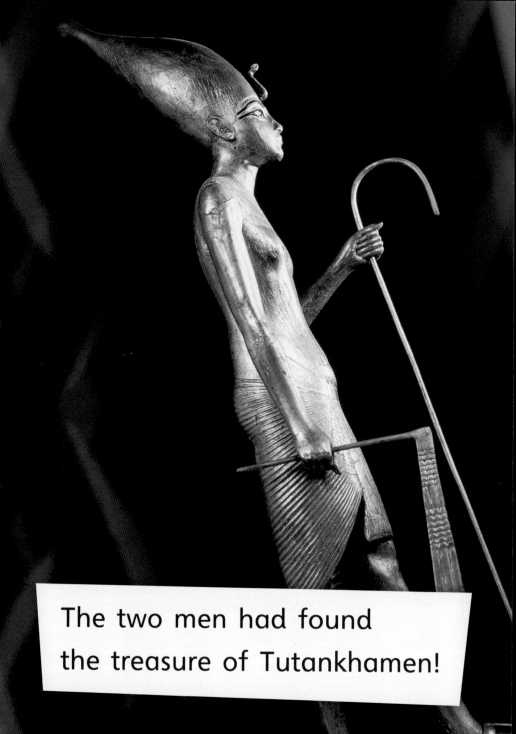

The two men had found
the treasure of Tutankhamen!

Quiz

Text Detective

- How long did it take the men to find the treasure?
- Would you have been scared to go in the tomb?

Word Detective

- **Phonic Focus:** Blending three phonemes
  Page 4: Sound out the word 'dug'.
  What sound is in the middle?
- Page 6: Find a word made of two words.
- Page 10: Find a word meaning 'discovered'.

Super Speller

Read these words:

then   two   all

Now try to spell them!

HA! HA! HA!

Q Why was the Egyptian boy crying?

A He wanted his mummy!

Before Reading

In this story

 Sir Bold

 Hal

 The king

 The princess

Tricky words

- notice
- marry
- princess
- forest
- hooray
- found

Introduce these tricky words and help the reader when they come across them later!

Story starter

Sir Bold was a poor knight who lived long ago. He had a faithful servant called Hal and an old horse called Flash. One day, they saw a notice about a lost gold cup. Whoever found the cup could marry the princess.

Sir Bold
and the
Gold Cup

Sir Bold read the notice.
"I will find that gold cup and marry the princess!" he said.

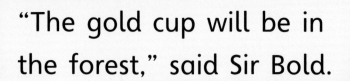

"The gold cup will be in the forest," said Sir Bold.

"The gold cup will be in the sand," said Hal.

They came to the forest.

"I will look here," said Sir Bold.

But the gold cup was not there.

They came to the sand.
"I will dig here," said Hal.

"The cup will not be there," said Sir Bold.

"Yes, it will," said Hal, "and I will marry the princess."

"There is the gold cup!" said Hal.

But Sir Bold got the cup.

"Hooray!" said Sir Bold.

"Now I can marry the princess!"

"I found the cup," said Hal.

"But I got it out of the sand," said Sir Bold.

Sir Bold took the cup to
the king.

"You can marry the princess,"
said the king.

Sir Bold looked at the princess.
"Will you marry me?"
said Sir Bold.

"No, thank you," said the princess. "I want to marry Hal!"

What do you think Sir Bold is thinking now?

Quiz

HA! HA! HA!

Q What fruit do you find on gold coins?

A Dates.